A SPECIAL GIFT FOR READERS

I prepared a simple and helpful checklist you can download that gives you a list of common defenses that you might assert in response to a copyright infringement claim. You can access this checklist by visiting this website:

NickGuinn.com/resources

FREE DOWNLOAD

DON'T COPY & PASTE

WHAT TO DO WHEN YOU ARE SUED FOR COPYRIGHT INFRINGEMENT

NICK GUINN

CORALREEFIP
A Community for Innovators, Inventors, and Entrepreneurs

PUBLISHED BY CORAL REEF IP

Print book ISBN: 978-1-957969-02-2
eBook ISBN: 978-1-957969-03-9

#####

While all attempts have been made to verify the information provided in this book, neither the author nor the publisher assumes any responsibility for errors, omissions or contradictory interpretations of the subject matter herein. This publication is designed to provide accurate and authoritative information with regard to the subject matter covered. The purchaser or reader of this publication assumes responsibility for the use of these materials and information. Adherence to all applicable laws and regulations, including federal, state, and local, governing professional licensing, business practices, advertising, and any other aspects of doing business is the sole responsibility of the reader.

Coral Reef IP publishes books for business owners, officers, and legal counsel to protect, commercialize, enforce, and defend their intellectual property. I offer a painless process enabling readers to benefit from the authority that comes from practicing and teaching intellectual property law. Do you have intellectual property that you wish to protect, commercialize, enforce, or defend?

Visit NickGuinn.com for more details.

CONTENTS

For Kristen, the love of my life. May we continue on each of life's adventures, together forever.

SPECIAL THANKS

I would like to express my heartfelt gratitude to my clients who trust me with their legal matters. These individuals and businesses have been the cornerstone of my professional journey. Each case, each challenge, and each success has contributed to the insights and experiences shared in this book. The confidence these clients place in me provides a constant source of motivation to excel in the complex field of copyright law.

I also owe an immense debt of gratitude to my mentor, friend, and managing partner, John Cave. His guidance has been instrumental in shaping my approach to the law. John has taught me the invaluable skill of evaluating client problems with a laser focus on the clients themselves, their unique goals, and the ability to help them perform cost-benefit analyses. His wisdom has not only made me a better lawyer but has also deeply influenced the practical, client-centered approach advocated in this book. I am thankful for John's unwavering support and for his example of what it means to be not just a great lawyer, but a true counselor to our clients.

PART 1

WELCOME

WHY IS THE INFORMATION IN THIS BOOK IMPORTANT?

Understanding how to navigate copyright issues is important for businesses. Copyright infringement claims can arise unexpectedly, and the consequences can be severe, including costly lawsuits, reputational damage, and significant financial penalties. This book provides guidance on how to respond to demand letters and lawsuits, helping businesses mitigate risks and avoid common pitfalls. By equipping yourself with the knowledge contained in this book, you can proactively protect your business, make informed decisions, and comply with copyright laws.

The information in this book is not just about reacting to problems but also about preventing them. This book empowers you with practical tools and strategies to maintain a sound operation, fostering a culture of respect for intellectual property. In an environment where copyright issues are increasingly prevalent, the insights provided here are invaluable for any business aiming to thrive without the burden of legal disputes.

WHO SHOULD READ THIS BOOK?

This book is intended for business owners, managers, and entrepreneurs who conduct business online. Whether you run a small startup or manage a large corporation, understanding how to respond to copyright demand letters and lawsuits is important for protecting your business. Preventing demand letters and lawsuits is equally, if not more important.

Marketing professionals, content creators, and anyone involved in producing or using creative works will also find this guide helpful in establishing lawful practices and in avoiding copyright infringement. If you are looking for answers to one or more of the following questions, then this book is for you.

1. What should I do if I receive a copyright demand letter?
2. What are some defenses against copyright infringement claims?
3. What steps should I take if I am sued for copyright infringement?
4. How can I negotiate a settlement for a copyright dispute?
5. What preventive measures can I implement to avoid future copyright issues?

The answers to these questions are based on my experience. Different lawyers may offer different strategies.

WHY I WROTE THIS BOOK

As an intellectual property lawyer, I see the stress that copyright issues cause businesses. Over the years, I have worked with numerous clients who were blindsided by demand letters or lawsuits, unsure of how to respond or protect their interests. These experiences highlight a significant gap in accessible, practical information for business owners and managers dealing with copyright infringement. I wrote this book to fill that gap, providing a guide to help businesses navigate these challenges.

One of the main reasons I wrote this book is to empower business owners with the knowledge needed to make informed decisions. Copyright law can be intimidating, and many businesses find themselves on the wrong side of it simply because they lack understanding. By demystifying the legal processes and offering practical advice, I aim to equip readers with the tools to handle copyright issues.

Another motivation for writing this book was to promote a culture of respect for intellectual property. In today's digital age, where content is easily shared and reproduced, it is more important than ever for businesses to understand the value of creative works and the legal implications of using them. By educating readers on best practices for copyright compliance, I hope to foster a greater appreciation for intellectual property and encourage ethical business practices. Ultimately, this book is about helping businesses thrive without the burden of legal disputes, ensuring they can focus on what they do best while respecting the rights of others.

This book is intended to provide general information about copyright infringement issues. It is important to note that the information contained herein is not a substitute for personalized legal advice from a qualified attorney. Copyright law is complex and constantly evolving, and each infringement case presents unique facts and circumstances that require individualized analysis.

While this book offers insights and practical tips, it cannot account for the specific nuances of your specific situation. Readers should use this information as a starting point for understanding copyright infringement matters but should consult with an attorney before taking any action. The author and publisher disclaim any liability for actions taken or not taken based solely on the contents of this book.

PART 2

CHAPTERS

COPYRIGHT BASICS

In today's digital age, understanding copyright law—even at a high level—is more important than ever. Whether you are creating your own content or using someone else's content, a solid grasp of copyright fundamentals can help you protect your assets and avoid costly legal disputes.

What is Copyright?

Copyright is a form of intellectual property protection granted to creators of original creative works. Think of it as a bundle of exclusive rights: the right to use, reproduce, distribute, perform, display, and even create new works based on the original. Why does this matter? Copyright is designed to encourage creativity by giving creators incentives to produce valuable works.[1]

Copyright is broad and it covers literary works, including software code, musical compositions and recordings, dramatic works and choreography, pictorial, graphic, and sculptural works, audiovisual productions like movies and video games, and even architectural works, to name a few. Here is an important distinction to keep in mind. Copyright protects the expression of ideas, not the ideas themselves. While a specific blog post about business strategies is protected, the general concepts behind the business strategy are not likely protected by copyright.

---

[1] *See, e.g.*, U.S. CONST. art. I, § 8, cl. 8 ("The Congress shall have Power To . . . To promote the Progress of Science and useful Arts, by securing for limited Times to Authors and Inventors the exclusive Right to their respective Writings and Discoveries . . . .").

In the United States, copyright protection exists when a work is created and fixed in a tangible form—whether it is written down, recorded, or saved digitally. While registering a work with the U.S. Copyright Office is not mandatory for protection, it has benefits. These benefits include the ability to sue for infringement and potentially recover statutory damages and attorney's fees if you win a case.[2] Statutory damages and attorneys fees are often larger remedies than actual damages.

Copyright Ownership and Rights

When an original, creative work is created, its creator automatically becomes the copyright owner. Copyright ownership establishes several exclusive rights. You can make copies of the work, distribute it by

---

[2] 17 U.S.C. § 504.

selling, licensing, leveraging, performing it publicly (for certain types of works), displaying it publicly, and even creating new works based on the original.

There is a major exception to this concept that the creator owns the copyright: works made for hire.[3] Works made for hire treatment generally applies to works created by employees within the scope of their employment, and certain commissioned works, if agreed to in writing (prior to creation). In these scenarios, the employer or commissioning party owns the copyright, not the individual creator.

What Constitutes Copyright Infringement?

Copyright infringement occurs when someone uses a copyrighted work without

---

[3] 17 U.S.C. § 101.

the copyright owner's permission in a way that violates the owner's exclusive rights. This can occur in several ways:

- Direct infringement occurs when someone uses a copyrighted work without permission.
- Contributory infringement occurs when a party knowingly induces, causes, or materially contributes to copyright infringement by another.
- Vicarious infringement occurs when a party has the right and ability to supervise the infringing activity and also has a direct financial interest in such activities.

As a business owner, it is important to understand that you can be held liable not only for your own actions, but also for those of your employees or contractors acting within the scope of their employment or contract.

Fair Use Doctrine

The fair use doctrine allows limited use of copyrighted material without permission for purposes such as criticism, commentary, news reporting, teaching, scholarship, or research. However, determining fair use is not a simple exercise. Courts generally consider four factors:

1. The purpose and character of the use (including whether it is commercial or nonprofit educational).
2. The nature of the copyrighted work—whether it is factual or creative.
3. The amount and substantiality of the portion used in relation to the copyrighted work as a whole.
4. The effect of the use upon the potential market for or value of the copyrighted work.

The analysis may be straightforward if all four factors weigh for or against fair use.

However, if the factors split on different sides, the court may have a difficult decision to make.

In short, fair use is a complex concept. Many business owners fall into the trap of thinking any educational or non-profit use is automatically fair use, or that using a small portion of a work is always permitted. In reality, fair use determinations are made on a case-by-case basis, considering all four factors.

Digital Millennium Copyright Act

Copyright law has evolved, and the DMCA of 1998 reflects that evolution. For business owners, especially those with an online presence, two key provisions are particularly relevant:

1. Safe Harbor Provisions: These provisions protect online service providers from copyright

infringement liability for user-generated content. However, the online service provider must follow certain rules, including having a registered DMCA agent and a takedown policy.

2. Notice and Takedown Procedures: This process allows copyright owners to request the removal of infringing content from websites. This requirement is especially important for businesses that host user-generated content.

Common Copyright Myths

In the business world, several copyright myths persist. Here are a few examples:

1. MYTH: "If it is on the internet, it is free to use."

TRUTH: Works found online are often protected by copyright, just like physical works.

2. MYTH: "Giving credit is enough to avoid infringement."

   TRUTH: While attribution reflects good manners, it does not negate the need for permission or a license to use copyrighted work.

3. MYTH: "Changing 10% makes it a new work."

   TRUTH: There is no magic percentage that makes the use of copyrighted material permissible. Even small amounts of copying can be infringing.

4. MYTH: "We are a small business, so no one will notice."

   TRUTH: Small businesses can and do get sued for copyright violations. I have assisted numerous single-employee and single-owner businesses that have faced copyright infringement claims.

5. MYTH: "It is for a good cause, so it is okay."
   TRUTH: Non-profit or charitable use does not automatically qualify as fair use or exempt you from copyright laws. I routinely defend non-profits facing copyright infringement claims.

Understanding these myths can help you navigate copyright law more safely.

Conclusion

Copyright law is a complex but essential area for business owners to understand. By learning these fundamentals—what copyright protects, the rights it confers, what constitutes infringement, the fair use doctrine, and relevant digital-age legislation—you can better navigate the use of creative works in your business operations.

Remember, when in doubt about the use of copyrighted material, it is best to seek permission or consult with an attorney.

CEASE-AND-DESIST LETTERS

Imagine that you are going about your day when an official-looking letter lands on your desk, and you realize it is a cease-and-desist letter. It is a moment that can shake even the most seasoned business owner. Do not panic. Understanding these letters is your first step in resolving the situation. This chapter discusses the features of a typical cease-and-desist letter, helping you interpret its contents and assess your next steps with confidence.

Purpose and Function

A cease-and-desist letter is a letter sent to an individual or business demanding that it stop (cease) and refrain from continuing (desist) an allegedly unlawful activity. In the world of copyright infringement, these letters serve several important purposes.

First and foremost, they are designed to notify you of the alleged infringement. They also demand that you immediately stop the allegedly infringing activity. They usually request compensation for damages, and they often ask for large sums of money. Lastly, they often come with the threat of legal action if you don't meet the demands.

To be clear: a cease-and-desist letter is not a legal document filed with a court. It is a formal warning that a lawsuit might arise if you don't comply with the letter's demands. In many cases, these letters are used as a first step in resolving disputes without dragging the parties into litigation. It is often in everyone's interest to resolve the dispute at this stage.

Key Components

While the substance varies, most of these letters contain the same elements. The beginning of the letter usually contains the sender's information, often on an official letterhead. This includes the name, address, and contact information of the copyright holder or their legal representative.

Next, you will see your business name and address clearly stated. Sometimes the wrong party is identified. Pay close attention.

The date is prominently displayed, which is important as it may be referenced in future correspondence or legal proceedings.

The letter should state who owns the copyright to the work in question. This might be an individual or an entity.

You will find a description of the copyrighted work, including its title, registration number (if applicable), and a brief description. It is important that you know what work(s) are asserted. Sometimes, the sender asserts rights in an irrelevant work.

Pay special attention where the letter alleges how your business infringed on the copyright. This might include specific instances of infringement (like URLs where they found the infringing content), dates of the alleged infringement, and how they discovered the infringing use.

To give weight to their claim, the letter typically cites relevant copyright statutes.

Perhaps the most important section outlines what the sender wants you to do. Common demands include immediately ceasing all infringing activities, removing or destroying all infringing materials, providing an account of profits made from the infringing use, and paying damages or a licensing fee.

Often, the sender includes a deadline by which you must comply with these demands.

The letter usually concludes with a warning of potential legal consequences if you fail to meet the demands. The sender usually threatens litigation.

Assessing the Validity of the Claim

After you receive a cease-and-desist letter, it is important to assess the validity of the claim before you respond.

Start by verifying the copyright ownership. Has the sender provided proof that they actually own the copyright or that they have authority to send you the letter? You can search the U.S. Copyright Office's online database for registration information, if applicable. But remember, copyright exists from the moment of creation, so lack of registration does not necessarily mean the claim is invalid.

Next, evaluate the alleged infringement. Carefully compare the copyrighted work with your allegedly infringing use. It is like holding two pictures side by side and looking for differences and similarities. I have read letters asserting copyright infringement because my client published a photograph of a popular landmark, and the sender thought it was the same photograph. At best, the sender did not realize that my client's photo was different. At worst, the sender asserted a frivolous claim hoping that my client would not notice.

Consider whether your use might fall under fair use or another exception. Determine if you had permission or a license for the use.

Do not forget to consider possible defenses or exceptions. Fair use, as we discussed earlier, allows limited use of copyrighted material without permission for purposes such as criticism, comment, news reporting, teaching, scholarship, or research, when applicable. If you created your work independently without knowledge of the copyrighted work, that could be a valid defense. If the work is in the public domain, it is free for anyone to use.

Of course, verify how much time has passed. You might have a statute of limitations defense.

Red Flags and Warning Signs

While many cease-and-desist letters are legitimate, some may be questionable or even fraudulent. It is important to be on the lookout for red flags.

Watch out for vague or incorrect information. If the letter lacks specific details about the copyrighted work or the alleged infringement, or if there are errors in identifying your business or the work in question, it might be a sign that the claim is not well-founded.

Be wary of unreasonable demands or deadlines. Extremely short response times (i.e., 24—48 hours) or exorbitant monetary demands disproportionate to the alleged infringement could be signs of an illegitimate claim.[4]

Look out for a lack of professionalism. Poor grammar or spelling, unprofessional email addresses or letterhead can be signs that the letter is not coming from a reputable source.

---

[4] When applicable, statutory damages allow copyright claimants to receive damages between $750 and $30,000 per infringed work. That amount can be increased to $150,000 if the infringement was willful. Often, copyright claimants ask for $30,000, characterizing it as a compromise of their right to potentially recover $150,000. In these situations, $30,000 often far exceeds what the claimant would likely receive in federal court. To be clear, a demand for $30,000 does not necessarily signal an illegitimate claim. However, it is not necessarily the amount you should pay, if anything.

Finally, be alert for signs of copyright trolling. Mass-produced letters sent to multiple recipients, demands focused more on monetary settlement than on stopping infringement, or claims based on brief, common phrases or widely used images could indicate that you are dealing with a copyright troll.

If you notice these red flags, it does not necessarily mean the claim is invalid, but it does warrant extra caution and scrutiny. In such cases, it is particularly advisable to seek legal counsel before responding.

Initial Response Considerations

There are some initial considerations to keep in mind when you receive a cease-and-desist letter.

First and foremost, do not ignore it. Even if you believe the claim is without merit, ignoring a cease-and-desist letter can escalate the situation and potentially harm your legal position. Ignoring the letter can strengthen the claimant's position that the infringement was willful and increase the claimant's odds of recovering a higher damage award.

At the same time, do not panic. Remember that a cease-and-desist letter is not a lawsuit. You have time to assess the situation and formulate a response.

Preserve evidence immediately. Do not destroy relevant documents. This could be important if the matter proceeds to litigation.

Limit discussion of the letter to necessary parties (like your lawyer). Avoid public statements or admissions of guilt. Keep in mind that your statements can be used against you in litigation. Even your internal communications could be discovered during litigation. Think twice before sending your business partner an email that reads: "Oh gosh. We messed up. We going to be on the hook for $150,000."

Finally, consider seeking legal advice. Given the complexities of copyright law, it is often wise to consult with an experienced copyright lawyer.

Conclusion

A cease-and-desist letter is a serious matter. Understanding its components and purpose can help you navigate the situation more effectively. By carefully analyzing the letter's content, assessing the validity and strength of the claim, and considering your response options, you can take informed steps to protect your interests.

The next chapter discusses the initial steps you might take upon receiving a copyright claim, equipping you with the knowledge to handle this challenging situation with confidence and clarity.

WHAT TO DO WHEN YOU RECEIVE A CEASE-AND-DESIST LETTER

As a business owner, receiving a cease-and-desist letter can feel overwhelming. Your initial steps in response can significantly shape the outcome.

Initial Steps

When you receive a copyright demand, it is important to keep your cool. Whether it is a cease-and-desist letter or a more formal legal notice, your first steps should be measured and methodical.

Start by documenting the receipt. Note the date and time you received the claim. If it arrives via email, make sure it is saved and backed up. For physical mail, keep the envelope.

Take the time to read the entire claim carefully. Make sure you understand the allegations and demands.

Your first instinct might be to reach out to the claimant immediately to explain or apologize. Resist this impulse. Statements you make could potentially be used against you later.

Preserve relevant documents and inform key personnel about the claim. Stress the importance of not discussing the matter externally and limiting internal communications about the claim. Ideally, all communications will involve your attorney. Avoid making public statements or social media posts about the claim or discussing the claim with your friends at happy hour.

Remember, receiving a claim does not automatically mean you are at fault or that you will face legal action. It is the beginning of a process, and you have time to assess and handle it appropriately.

Preliminary Assessment

First, clearly identify the alleged infringement. What work is supposedly being infringed and how? Is it an image on your website? A portion of text in your marketing materials? A video on your social media?

Next, verify the timeline. When did the alleged infringement occur? How long has the content been in use? When did you first publish or use it? If enough time has passed, you might have a statute of limitations defense.

Try to trace the content's origin. Was it created in-house? Purchased from a stock image site? Commissioned from a freelancer? Did your employee copy and paste the image? This information is relevant in determining your position.

Identify the key personnel involved in creating, approving, or publishing the content in question. Their story(s) could be valuable as you move forward.

Finally, assess your potential exposure. Consider the scope of use. Has the allegedly infringing content been used in multiple places? Has it been central to any marketing campaigns? Understanding the extent of use will help you gauge potential liability. Similarly, does the claimant own a copyright registration? This fact could influence the plaintiff's potential recovery of damages. This exercise might be difficult without input from an experienced copyright lawyer.

This preliminary assessment is not about making judgments; it is about gathering facts. The clearer picture you have, the better prepared you will be for the next steps.

Preserving Evidence

Preserving evidence is almost always necessary, regardless of whether you believe the claim has merit. Proper documentation can be your lifeline if the matter escalates to litigation.

Start by implementing what is known as a "litigation hold." This is a directive to all relevant employees to preserve any documents or data that might be relevant to the claim. This includes emails related to the creation, acquisition, or use of the content, contracts or licenses related to the content, design files or drafts, and publication or upload logs.

Consider documenting the current state of affairs. If the allegedly infringing content is on your website or social media, you might take screenshots or screen recordings to document exactly how and where it appears. Before you create documents, consult with an attorney.

Do not forget about financial records. If the claim involves commercial use of the content, preserve records of any revenue that might be attributed to its use.

Consider maintaining a detailed chronology of events. When was the content created or acquired? When was it published? Log all subsequent events related to the claim. Again, consult with an attorney. An attorney is better positioned to help you carry out this exercise in a way that is privileged and minimizes the risk of needing to disclose during discovery.

Note, destroying or altering evidence after receiving a claim can have serious legal consequences. A judge might later instruct the jury to assume that you destroyed the documents. When in doubt, preserve it.

Seeking Legal Counsel

Consider consulting with, and retaining, a copyright attorney. An attorney will help, among other things, if you are unsure about the validity of the claim, if the allegedly infringing use is central to your business operations, if you receive a formal legal complaint rather than just a cease-and-desist letter, or if you are unsure about your rights or the strength of your position.

When choosing an attorney, look for someone specializing in intellectual property or copyright law. Consider their experience with cases similar to yours. Ask about their approach to resolving copyright disputes. And discuss their fee structure upfront.

Before your first consultation, gather all documents related to the claim, prepare a chronological summary of events, be ready to discuss your business's use of the content in question, and have a list of specific questions or concerns ready.

Attorney-client privilege only applies to communications with your lawyer. Usually, the privilege does not extend to internal discussions with your employees. Be mindful of this when discussing the case. An internal admission of fault could come back to haunt you during litigation.

Immediate Mitigation Steps

While you are assessing the situation and seeking advice, consider the following steps you might take to mitigate potential damages.

Consider temporarily removing the allegedly infringing content if it is easily removable, like an image on your website. However, consult with legal counsel before doing so, as this action could be seen as an act of wrongdoing in some circumstances.

If the content is being used in ongoing marketing campaigns or is scheduled for future use, consider pausing these activities until the matter is resolved.

Conduct a quick audit of your other content to see if there might be similar issues elsewhere. This can help you prevent additional claims.

In most cases, it is advisable to avoid making public statements about the claim. However, if the issue has already become public, consult with legal counsel about crafting an appropriate response.

Evaluate how removing the content or pausing its use might affect your business operations. Develop contingency plans if necessary.

Develop an Initial Response

As you gather information and consult with your team and attorney, you will need to start formulating your response strategy.

You might choose to comply fully with the claimant's requests if your assessment reveals that the claim is valid, and the demands are reasonable.

Often, there is room for negotiation, especially if you believe you have some valid defenses or if the demands are unreasonable.

If you believe the claim is without merit, you *might* choose to dispute it entirely. Unfortunately, the cost of litigation is significant, and the cost should factor into your decision.

Your choice will depend on various factors, including the strength of the claim, your potential liability, the importance of the content to your business, and your overall risk tolerance.

Research the Claimant

When faced with a copyright infringement claim, researching the claimant can provide valuable insight and inform your response strategy. One crucial aspect to investigate is whether the claimant frequently files copyright lawsuits. This information can be accessed from public court records, legal databases, and industry forums. A pattern of frequent filings might suggest that the claimant is engaged in copyright trolling—the practice of aggressively enforcing copyrights primarily to extract settlements rather than to protect creative works. Understanding this context can help you assess the claimant's motivations and potentially inform your negotiation strategy.

Consider two hypothetical copyright claimants. The first claimant has filed more than 200 lawsuits in the last three years. The other claimant has never filed a lawsuit. There is a good chance that the first claimant will file a lawsuit if you do not settle or dispel its accusations. The second claimant is less likely to sue, especially if the second claimant has a reputation for sending lots of demand letters. These are generalizations, of course, and should be treated accordingly.

It is also beneficial to analyze the claimant's litigation history to identify any patterns in their settlement behavior. Do they typically settle early in the proceedings, or do they tend to pursue cases through trial? Are there common settlement terms or amounts? This information can be gathered by examining court dockets, settlement agreements (if publicly available), and by consulting with other attorneys who may have dealt with this claimant before. Do not be surprised if third-parties are unwilling to discuss their settlement terms. If for no other reason, the settlement agreement might require confidentiality. Understanding the claimant's settlement tendencies can help you anticipate their likely moves and potentially expedite a resolution.

It is worth investigating whether the claimant has ever faced legal or ethical challenges related to their copyright enforcement practices. Have they been sanctioned by courts for frivolous lawsuits? Have they faced counterclaims for copyright misuse? Are there any public controversies or negative press surrounding their enforcement tactics? Such information can be found through legal news sources, court records, and sometimes general media coverage. If the claimant has a history of problematic behavior, this knowledge could guide your negotiations or legal strategy. However, it is crucial to verify any such information thoroughly and use it judiciously.

Conclusion

Receiving a copyright claim is a serious matter, but it does not need to be a crisis. By following these steps—documenting everything, conducting a thorough preliminary assessment, preserving evidence, managing internal communications, seeking appropriate legal counsel, taking immediate mitigation steps, and developing a response strategy—you will put yourself and your business in a better position.

Remember, each situation is unique, and this guide provides general considerations. The considerations in this book are not intended to substitute for legal advice tailored to your situation. Always consider seeking personalized legal counsel for your specific circumstances.

DEFENSE STRATEGIES

You took immediate steps to address a copyright claim. It is time to consider your legal options and develop a strategic response. This process can feel complex, but with guidance, you can chart a course that protects your interests.

Responding to the Claim

With your position assessed, it is time to craft your response. You need to be assertive in defending your rights while maintaining a professional tone that keeps the door open for settlement.

When crafting your response letter, address each point in the claim systematically. If you are disputing the claim, provide evidence supporting your position. If appropriate, suggest a resolution or next steps. Remember, your initial response can set the tone for subsequent interactions, so it is often beneficial to have legal counsel review your response before sending it.

It is important to acknowledge receipt of the claim without admitting fault. Confirm that you received the claim. State that you are investigating the matter. However, avoid admitting fault or making promises at this stage.

If the claim lacks specifics, do not hesitate to request more detailed information. Ask for evidence of copyright ownership if it was not provided. If the claimant alleges that the copyright is registered, ask for a copy of the copyright registration and application deposit. Seek clarification on any ambiguous points in the claim. The more information you have, the better equipped you will be to respond effectively.

Negotiation Strategies

In many cases, negotiation can be an effective way to resolve copyright disputes without resorting to litigation.

Start by setting realistic goals. Determine your best-case and worst-case scenarios. Identify your "walk away" point—the least favorable terms you would accept. This preparation will help you navigate the negotiation process more effectively.

If the demands are unreasonable, be prepared with counteroffers. Consider non-monetary solutions, such as attribution or limited future use rights. Sometimes, creative solutions can satisfy both parties' interests.

Effective communication is key in negotiations. Listen actively to understand the other party's concerns. Focus on interests rather than positions to find mutually beneficial solutions.

Be aware that some copyright claimants only want money. Identifying these claimants early and carefully developing your strategy will help you best position yourself.

Throughout the negotiation process, keep detailed records of communications with the claimant or its counsel.[5] and confirm any agreements in writing. This documentation can be invaluable if there are any misunderstandings later.

---

[5] Several copyright claimants use third-party services to serve copyright demands. By way of example, you might receive a demand from such a third-party service asking for $500. If the matter is not resolved at this stage—or you do not dispel the claimant's allegations—the claimant might escalate the matter to litigation. At that point, you will hear from a lawyer or a law firm representing the claimant, and the lawyer will likely ask for more than the original $500.

Remember, successful negotiation often involves finding a middle ground that addresses both parties' concerns.

Settlement Considerations

Sometimes, settling the claim may be the most prudent course of action. It is like choosing to end a chess game with a draw—you might not win outright, but you avoid a potentially costly defeat.

Like you, the claimant has several considerations including the following:

- Do you have money to pay the claimant?
- Do you have enough money to pay the claimant even more money?
- Do you have defenses that could complicate the claimant's efforts?
- How much money will it cost to file a lawsuit (e.g., filing fees; attorney's fees)?

- How much money will it cost to take a case all the way to trial?
- Can the claimant recover its attorney's fees?
- Do you have the money to pay the claimant's attorney's fees?
- How much money will a court likely award in damages?

Settling has its advantages. You can avoid costly and time-consuming litigation, maintain control over the outcome, potentially preserve business relationships, and resolve the issue quickly and confidentially. However, it also has potential drawbacks. It may involve paying damages or licensing fees, could be seen as an admission of wrongdoing, and might encourage other potential claimants.

There are various types of settlement agreements to consider. You might agree to a one-time payment, arrange for proper licensing for past and/or future use, agree to remove and cease use of the copyrighted material, or some combination of these.

When negotiating settlement terms, push for a non-admission clause to avoid admitting liability. Request confidentiality if you want to prevent public disclosure. Try to secure a release from future claims related to the same use. If agreeing to content removal, negotiate a reasonable timeframe.

Have legal counsel review any settlement agreement before signing. Remember, a well-negotiated settlement is often the most cost-effective and business-friendly resolution to a copyright claim.

When to Litigate

Sometimes litigation is necessary. When considering litigation, weigh several factors. How strong is your case? Do you have strong defenses or counterclaims? Are the potential damages significant enough to justify litigation? Could a favorable ruling benefit your business in the long term? Do you have the time and financial resources for a potentially lengthy legal battle?

Understanding the potential costs is important. Litigation can be expensive, often costing tens or hundreds of thousands of dollars. It can drag on for months or years, requiring significant time and attention from key personnel.

The discovery process of gathering and producing evidence can be burdensome (e.g., time, stress, money). And if you lose the lawsuit, you may have to pay the claimant significant damages.

A typical copyright lawsuit follows a predictable timeline: filing of the complaint, responding to the complaint, conducting the discovery phase (often the longest and most costly part), briefing pre-trial motions, going to trial (if the case isn't settled or dismissed), and dealing with potential appeals.

Be aware that you might file counterclaims, and consider potential vulnerabilities. Remember, the decision to litigate should not be taken lightly. Always consult with experienced copyright counsel before proceeding.

Alternative Dispute Resolution

In addition to litigation, parties can pursue several alternative dispute resolution (ADR) methods. ADR often provides faster, less expensive, and more flexible solutions.

Mediation is one popular ADR method. A neutral third party (mediator) helps facilitate a mutually agreeable solution. It is a non-binding process, giving parties control over the final agreement. Mediation is often faster and less expensive than litigation and can help preserve business relationships. Timing, the information available to the parties, and most importantly, the willingness of the parties, often dictates the success of mediation.

Arbitration is another option. In arbitration, a neutral third party (arbitrator) hears both sides and makes a decision. It can be binding or non-binding, depending on the agreement. Arbitration is often faster and less formal than court proceedings and typically offers more privacy than litigation.

The Copyright Claims Board (CCB) is a three-member tribunal. It was established in 2020. It operates within the U.S. Copyright Office and provides a streamlined, cost-effective alternative to federal court for resolving copyright disputes involving claims up to $30,000. Both parties must agree (i.e., opt-in) to participate. The CCB handles various copyright issues, including infringement claims, declarations of non-infringement, and certain DMCA-related disputes. The proceedings are primarily conducted online, making it more accessible than traditional court litigation. While CCB decisions are binding, they have limited precedential value and cannot be cited in other CCB proceedings or federal court cases.

When deciding whether to pursue ADR, consider the nature of your relationship with the copyright holder, the complexity of the dispute, and your desired outcomes.

Conclusion

Responding to a copyright claim involves carefully weighing various legal options and strategies. Whether you choose to negotiate, settle, litigate, or pursue alternative dispute resolution, your decision should be based on a thorough assessment of your position, potential costs and benefits, and long-term business implications.

Remember, each situation is unique, and strategies that work in one case may not be appropriate in another. Always consult with experienced legal counsel to tailor your approach to your specific circumstances.

It is important to consider what happens when negotiation and alternative dispute resolution fail. The next chapter discusses the scenario where you find yourself facing a copyright infringement lawsuit. Understanding this process will further equip you to navigate a copyright dispute.

COPYRIGHT INFRINGEMENT LAWSUITS

Despite our best efforts, litigation is sometimes inevitable. Knowledge is power, and understanding the process can help you navigate litigation efficiently.

Litigation at a Glance

Although every case is unique, litigation follows an established sequence. A lawsuit begins when the plaintiff (i.e., the copyright holder) files a complaint in federal court.[6] Among other things, the complaint alleges facts supporting the plaintiff's theory of

---

[6] Copyright infringement claims take place exclusively in federal court. 28 U.S. Code § 1338(a).

infringement and what remedy(s) the plaintiff is seeking.

Next, you will receive a summons and a copy of the complaint through a process called "service." This formal notification often arrives via personal delivery. It is more than a mere formality: it determines your deadline to respond.

Once served, you have a limited time (usually 21 days) to respond. This deadline is important. Failing to respond can result in a default judgment against you, essentially handing victory to the plaintiff without a fight.[7]

If you respond,[8] the case moves into the discovery phase. This is where both parties

---

[7] When the plaintiff asks the Court to enter a default judgment (i.e., victory because the defendant did not file an answer), the plaintiff will ask for a large damage award. Because the defendant is not there to defend itself, the Court may award higher damages than if the defendant appeared and defended the lawsuit.

[8] You have several options: you can file an answer wherein you admit or deny the various allegations contained in the complaint; or you can move to dismiss

exchange relevant information, which can include documents, depositions, and written questions called interrogatories. It is a fact-finding mission that often feels invasive, but it is a critical part of building your case.

Before the trial, either party can file various motions to resolve issues. These might include motions to dismiss the case or for summary judgment. If these don't resolve the matter, and you don't settle, you are going to trial, which could be decided by a jury or a judge.

Even after the trial, the dispute is not necessarily over. The losing party may file an appeal, while the winning party seeks to enforce the judgment.

---

the complaint for one of several reasons (e.g., the complaint does not contain enough facts to notify the defendant; the venue and/or jurisdiction are improper; etc.).

Understanding this roadmap can help you prepare for what is ahead and make informed decisions at each turn.

Steps After Service

Being served with a lawsuit can be jarring. Do not panic. Being sued does not mean you lost. Rather, it is the beginning of a legal process.

Take note of the response deadline specified in the summons. Mark this date prominently and ensure you do not miss it. Missing this deadline leads to default, which gives the plaintiff an easy win.

Retain a lawyer if you have not already done so.[9] Look for a lawyer experienced in copyright litigation. Once you find your lawyer, provide them with all relevant

---

[9] Individuals can represent themselves *pro se* but legal entities (e.g., limited liability companies; corporations; etc.) must be represented by licensed attorneys.

documents and information. The more they know, the better they can defend you.

Implement what is called a "litigation hold" immediately. This means stopping any routine document destruction and informing all relevant employees to preserve any potentially relevant documents or data. In the digital age, this preservation is important.

Do not forget to check your insurance policies. Some business insurance policies cover copyright infringement claims. If applicable, notify your insurer promptly to avoid jeopardizing potential coverage.

Lastly, resist the urge to discuss the lawsuit. Loose lips sink ships, as they say.

The Strength of the Plaintiff's Case

Evaluate the strength of the plaintiff's case. Identify each specific allegation of infringement and note any factual errors or misrepresentations.

Next, evaluate the validity of the copyright itself. Is the work actually protected by copyright? Has it been properly registered? These are important questions that could make or break the case. They might also impact the plaintiff's remedies.

Ownership is another critical factor. Can the plaintiff prove it owns the copyright? Are there any issues with the chain of title? Sometimes, the person crying foul is not actually the rightful owner of the copyright.

Consider potential defenses. Does your use potentially qualify as fair use? Are there other applicable defenses, such as having a license or having created your work independently?

Finally, examine the potential damages. What type of damages is the plaintiff seeking (or entitled to): statutory or actual?

Are there grounds to limit or mitigate these damages? Understanding the potential financial impact can help inform your strategy moving forward.

This assessment is not just an academic exercise. It will shape your litigation strategy and help you make informed decisions about whether to settle or proceed to trial.

Settling Versus Defending

Even after a lawsuit is filed, settlement remains an option. In fact, settlement remains an option throughout the lawsuit, including a potential appeal. How do you decide whether to settle or fight? It is a decision that requires careful consideration.

Start with a thorough cost-benefit analysis. Estimate the total cost of litigation, including legal fees, time investment, and potential damages. Compare this to the cost of potential settlement offers. Often, the numbers make the decision clear.

Consider the broader business implications, too. How might protracted litigation affect your operations and reputation? Could a public trial expose sensitive business information? These factors might not show up directly on the balance sheet, but they are important considerations.

Evaluate your chances of success based on your earlier assessment of the case. Remember, even strong cases can be unpredictable in court. There is always an element of risk.

Assess any settlement offers on the table. Are the terms reasonable? How do they compare to your best and worst-case litigation outcomes?

Do not forget to consider the long-term consequences. How might the outcome affect your future business practices? Could settling encourage or discourage future claims against you? Think beyond the immediate case to your broader business strategy.

Remember, the decision to settle or litigate is not set in stone until a judgment is entered. You can continue to explore settlement options throughout the litigation process. Keep an open mind and be ready to pivot if circumstances change.

Developing Your Legal Strategy

It is time to develop a legal strategy. Start by deciding how to respond to the complaint. Will you file an answer, a motion to dismiss, or another type of response? If you are answering, you will need to respond to each allegation and assert any affirmative defenses. Will you contact the other side beforehand?

Consider whether you have any valid counterclaims against the plaintiff. Common counterclaims include seeking a declaratory judgment of non-infringement or invalidity, or alleging copyright misuse.

Plan your discovery strategy. What information will you seek from the plaintiff? Prepare for depositions, document production, and written discovery. This is your chance to gather ammunition for your defense.

Develop your key legal arguments. Whether it is fair use, lack of substantial similarity, or another defense, identify the main points of your legal position. Find key cases and statutes that support you.

Consider strategic motions, such as a motion for summary judgment. Be prepared to respond to motions filed by the plaintiff as well. Be aware that missing deadlines, improperly relying on evidence, or otherwise failing to follow "the rules" can be fatal.

Although trial is unlikely, operate under the assumption that your case will proceed to trial. For example, request documents during discovery as if you will need those documents during trial. If the case goes to trial, plan your trial strategy. What is your narrative? What key evidence will you present? Consider whether you will need expert witnesses.

Throughout litigation, keep settlement considerations in mind. Determine your settlement parameters and consider the timing of any settlement overtures. For example, making a settlement offer shortly before the plaintiff deposes you or one of your witnesses might signal to the plaintiff that you do not want the plaintiff to discover harmful evidence.

Remember, your strategy should be flexible. Be ready to adapt as the case develops and new information comes to light.

Potential Defenses

Understanding potential defenses is important when developing your strategy. In copyright infringement cases, several common defenses might apply to your situation.

Fair use is a common defense. You might argue that your use falls under this doctrine, which involves analyzing four factors: the purpose and character of your use, the nature of the copyrighted work, the amount used, and the effect on the potential market for the original work.

You might also argue that there is no substantial similarity between your work and the copyrighted work. This often involves a detailed comparison and sometimes requires expert testimony.

Independent creation is another potential defense. If you can show that you created your work independently, without access to or knowledge of the plaintiff's work, you might be in the clear.

Perhaps you had a license or authorization to use the work. If you can prove you had permission, either through a formal license or other authorization, that is a strong defense.

You might challenge the validity of the plaintiff's copyright itself. This could involve arguing a lack of originality or failure to comply with copyright formalities.

The statute of limitations might apply if the plaintiff waited too long to bring the claim. In copyright cases, this is typically three years. Be aware of the discovery rule.

You might argue misuse of copyright, claiming that the plaintiff has misused their copyright in a way that violates public policy.

Keep in mind that the defenses listed here are not exhaustive.

The specific defenses available will depend on the facts of your case. Your attorney can help you identify and develop the most appropriate defenses for your situation.

Conclusion

Facing a copyright infringement lawsuit is undoubtedly a serious matter. But with proper preparation and a strong legal strategy, you can navigate the process effectively. Remember that litigation is often unpredictable, and staying flexible in your approach is helpful. Always work closely with experienced copyright counsel to make informed decisions at each stage of the process.

The next chapter delves deeper into what you can expect if your case proceeds to trial.

The chapter explores the role of expert witnesses, walks through the trial process itself, and discusses potential outcomes.

TRIAL

A copyright infringement trial is the culmination of many months, if not years, of litigation. It can feel intimidating. However, understanding the key aspects will help you navigate it with greater confidence.

Overview of the Trial Process

Trial begins with jury selection, also known as *voir dire* (if it is a jury trial).[10] Potential jurors are questioned to ensure an unbiased panel. Both sides can challenge potential jurors, either for cause or using peremptory challenges.

---

[10] A trial tried to a judge (i.e., without a jury) is referred to as a "bench trial."

Once the jury is empaneled (in a jury trial), the trial proceeds to opening statements. This is your first chance to tell your story to the jury, framing the narrative of your defense. It is an important moment to make a strong first impression.

Next comes the plaintiff's case. The copyright holder will present its evidence and witnesses, attempting to prove infringement. Your lawyer will have the opportunity to cross-examine these witnesses, poking holes in their case where possible.

After the plaintiff rests, you have an opportunity to present your case-in-chief. As the defendant, you will present your evidence and witnesses to refute the claims and prove your defenses. Be prepared for the plaintiff's lawyer to cross-examine you and your witnesses.

The plaintiff may then present a rebuttal, offering additional evidence to counter your defense. This back-and-forth culminates in closing arguments, where both sides summarize their cases and make their final pleas to the jury.

Before deliberation begins, the judge will instruct the jury on the law and how to apply it. Then, the jury will exit the courtroom to discuss the case privately and reach a verdict.

This entire process can last anywhere from a single day to several weeks (or even months), depending on the complexity of your case.

Using Discovery at Trial

The discovery phase in a copyright infringement case plays a crucial role in shaping the trial strategy and presentation of evidence. During discovery, both parties gather information, documents, and testimony that can aid in proving or defending against claims of infringement.

One of the primary uses of discovery during trial is to establish the facts surrounding the alleged infringement. Through document requests and interrogatories, parties can obtain evidence of the creation, ownership, and registration of the copyrighted work, as well as details about the allegedly infringing use. This information forms the foundation of each party's case and can be presented as exhibits or referenced in witness testimony during the trial.

Depositions taken during discovery often play a significant role in trial proceedings. Testimony from key witnesses, including the copyright holder, alleged infringer, and any relevant third parties, can be used to support arguments or challenge the credibility of witnesses. Deposition transcripts may be read into the record if a witness is unavailable for trial, or used to impeach a witness whose trial testimony contradicts their earlier statements.

Expert witness reports and depositions, typically obtained during discovery, are critical in copyright trials. Among other things, experts can be used to establish or contest substantial similarity between works, assess damages, or provide industry-specific information. The opinions and analyses of these experts often form a cornerstone of each party's case.

Discovery efforts can also yield evidence that supports or refutes various defenses, such as fair use, independent creation, or prior art. For instance, documents showing the defendant's creative process might support a claim of independent creation, while evidence of the plaintiff's licensing practices could influence a fair use analysis and potential damages.

Additionally, financial records and market data obtained during discovery are crucial for determining damages. This information can be used to calculate damages.

Lastly, admissions made during discovery, whether in response to requests for admission or during depositions, can be powerful tools at trial. These admissions can streamline the presentation of evidence and sometimes decisively influence the outcome of specific issues.

In sum, the thorough and strategic use of information gathered during discovery can significantly shape the narrative presented at trial, support or undermine key arguments, and ultimately influence the court's decision in a copyright infringement case.

The Role of Expert Witnesses

Generally speaking, witnesses cannot testify regarding their opinions. Expert witnesses, however, are an exception to this general rule.

There are various types of experts you might call upon. Subject matter experts, like photographers in a photography copyright case, can speak to the nuances of their field. Damages experts can assess the economic effects of alleged infringement, which is important for determining what you might be required to pay if the plaintiff you are found liable. And in cases involving digital works, forensic experts can provide technical analysis.

When selecting an expert, look for relevant expertise and experience testifying in similar cases. They should be able to explain complex concepts clearly to a jury. Vet their background thoroughly to preempt any challenges to their credibility. You might inquire whether an expert has been prevented from testifying in the past, and if so, why.

After you choose your expert, work closely with them to develop their report and testimony. Prepare them for cross-examination and ensure their testimony aligns with your overall case strategy.

Do not forget to scrutinize the plaintiff's experts as well. Challenge their qualifications and methodologies, and prepare effective cross-examination questions to undermine their credibility or conclusions if necessary.

Possible Outcomes and Business Implications

As the trial concludes, it is important to understand the potential outcomes and what they might mean for your business.

Your best-case scenario is often a finding of no infringement. This clears you of the claims, and you might be able to recover some legal costs.

By contrast, a finding of infringement means you will need to cease the infringing use and may have to pay damages and/or attorney's fees. This could significantly impact your business operations, so plan accordingly.

Specifically, the court may issue an injunction, ordering you to stop using the copyrighted material. This could require changes to your products, services, or marketing materials. Have a plan in place for how you will comply while minimizing business disruption.

Monetary damages come in two flavors: actual damages based on the copyright owner's losses or your profits from the infringement on the one hand, and statutory damages ranging from $750 to

$30,000 per work (or up to $150,000 for willful infringement) on the other. Consider the potential financial impact and plan for payment if necessary.

Do not forget about attorney's fees and costs. You may have to pay the plaintiff's legal fees, which can significantly increase the financial impact of an adverse judgment.

Appeals

If the verdict does not go your way, you might consider an appeal. This process has its own set of rules and considerations.[11]

Grounds for appeal typically include legal errors by the court (such as incorrect jury instructions), improperly admitted or excluded evidence, or lack of sufficient evidence to support the verdict (e.g., the

---

[11] Conversely, the other side might file an appeal.

plaintiff did not show that the allegedly infringing work was a copy of or substantially similar to the copyrighted work). Remember, you generally cannot introduce new evidence on appeal. You are limited to arguing that the trial court made an error.

As with trials, timing is important in appeals. You must typically file a notice of appeal within thirty (30) days of the judgment. However, the entire process can take a year or more.

Potential outcomes of an appeal include affirming the original decision, reversing it, or remanding the case back to the lower court for further proceedings.

While your appeal is pending, you may need to comply with the trial court's judgment. Weigh the costs and benefits of pursuing an appeal carefully, and be prepared for the possibility of settlement negotiations during this process.

Conclusion

Navigating a copyright infringement trial is not intuitive, but understanding what to expect can help you prepare effectively and make informed decisions. Remember, each case is unique, so always work closely with your attorney and be ready to adapt your strategy as the case unfolds.

The next chapter discusses steps that you might take to protect your business from future copyright infringement claims. This proactive approach can help you avoid the courtroom in the future.

COPYRIGHT COMPLIANCE POLICIES

As a business owner or manager, you should develop and implement copyright compliance policies. These policies will help you defend against future legal challenges and foster a culture of respect for intellectual property within your organization.

Developing a Copyright Policy

A copyright compliance policy should be a living document that evolves with your business and the legal landscape. Start by outlining clear guidelines on the use of copyrighted materials, procedures for obtaining permissions and licenses, rules for creating and using original content, protocols for responding to infringement allegations, and consequences for policy violations.

Remember, one size does not fit all. Tailor your policy to your specific business needs. Consider the unique risks and practices in your industry, and address the different types of content your business creates or uses, whether it is text, images, videos, or software, etc. Your policy should provide guidance for both internal use and public-facing content.

Ensure your copyright policy aligns with your existing company policies. Review your social media, marketing, and IT policies for consistency, and update related policies to reference your new copyright policy. This alignment ensures a cohesive approach to compliance across your organization.

Finally, do not forget to ask your attorney to review the policy. Plan to update the policy regularly to reflect changes in copyright law and your business practices.

Guidelines for Employees

Your employees are on the front lines of copyright compliance. Equip them with clear, actionable guidelines. Start by defining what constitutes acceptable use of copyrighted materials. Dispel myths and clarify misconceptions about fair use and online content use.

Establish step-by-step procedures for obtaining and documenting permissions. Provide templates for permission requests and set up a central repository for storing licenses and permissions. This makes it easy for employees to do the right thing.

Address common scenarios your employees might encounter. Provide guidance on using images found online, explain proper source attribution, and discuss the use of content on social media platforms. The more specific and relevant your guidelines, the easier it will be for your team to follow them.

Training Staff on Proper Image Use

A policy is only effective if it is understood and followed. Regular training is essential to ensure your copyright policy does not gather dust on a shelf. Design engaging, interactive training sessions that use real-world examples and case studies. If necessary, tailor your training to different departments. What the marketing team needs to know might be different from the IT department.

Conduct initial training for all new employees, followed by refresher courses over time. Be prepared to offer additional training when copyright laws change or after any incidents. Be careful, however, as what you say can be used in litigation.

Address common misconceptions and questions in your training. Debunk myths about online content use, provide a FAQ section in your training materials, and encourage employees to ask questions and seek clarification. The more comfortable your team is with the subject, the more likely they are to comply.

Approval Processes for Content

A robust approval process can catch potential infringement before it occurs, saving you from costly legal battles down the line. Create a clear content review workflow, establishing a chain of review for all published content. Implement checklists for copyright compliance and use project management tools to track the review process.

Designate specific individuals or roles responsible for copyright clearance. Ensure these individuals receive advanced copyright training. For complex issues, consider creating a copyright compliance team.

Implement checklists for different types of content, such as blog posts, marketing materials, and product descriptions. Include items like source verification, and permission status. Regularly update these checklists based on new laws or company experiences.

Establish a final review process before content goes live. Consider using software tools to scan for potential copyright issues. Document the final approval for each piece of content.

Documenting Copyright Ownership and Licenses

Proper documentation is important for managing your own copyrights and tracking usage rights. Maintain detailed records of all original works created by your company, documenting the creation process, including who created the work and when. For important works, consider registering them with the Copyright Office.

Implement a system for tracking usage rights. Create a database of all licensed content, including key information like license terms, expiration dates, and usage restrictions. Implement a system for tracking content use across your organization.

Conduct periodic audits of your website, marketing materials, and other content. Verify that all content is either original, properly licensed, or falls under fair use. Address any compliance issues promptly.

If your business deals with user-generated content, develop clear policies for handling it. Implement systems to monitor and moderate user content, and have a process for responding to takedown requests.

Fostering a Culture of Respect

Creating a company culture that values intellectual property rights is important for long-term compliance. Promote ethical content use as a company value, including respect for intellectual property in your company's core values. Lead by example, with management demonstrating proper content use. Recognize and reward employees who consistently adhere to copyright policies.

Encourage employees to report potential violations by establishing a clear, non-retaliatory reporting process. Ensure all reports are taken seriously and investigated promptly. Be aware that such communications could be discoverable during litigation. Discuss attorney-client privilege and related issues with an experienced copyright attorney.

Include copyright compliance in performance reviews, offer incentives for employees who suggest improvements to copyright practices, and publicly acknowledge teams or individuals who excel in copyright compliance.

Integrate copyright awareness into daily operations. Include copyright reminders in content creation tools and templates, make copyright resources easily accessible to all employees, and regularly communicate about copyright issues and best practices.

Conclusion

Implementing robust copyright compliance policies is essential for protecting your business from infringement claims and fostering a culture of respect for intellectual property. By developing clear guidelines, providing thorough training, establishing approval processes, maintaining proper documentation, and staying updated on legal developments, you can significantly reduce your risk of copyright infringement.

Remember that copyright compliance is an ongoing process. Regularly review and update your policies, continue to educate your team, and be prepared to adapt to new challenges as technology and the law evolve. With diligence and commitment, you can turn copyright compliance from a legal necessity into a competitive advantage, demonstrating your business's integrity and respect for creativity.

The next chapter discusses best practices for digital asset management. This will help you effectively source, use, and track copyrighted materials in your business operations, further strengthening your copyright compliance efforts.

DIGITAL ASSET MANAGEMENT

Today, businesses rely heavily on visual content to engage audiences and convey their messages effectively. However, this reliance on images comes with a significant risk: the potential for copyright infringement. As a business owner or manager, understanding how to properly source, manage, and use digital assets, particularly images, is important to minimizing this risk.[12]

---

[12] Each year, thousands of lawsuits are filed in the United States based on photographs that are copied and pasted to websites and social media platforms. That figure does not account for the disputes that are resolved short of litigation.

Image Licenses

Before you use an image in your marketing materials, website, or any other business content, it is important to understand the type of license it carries (if any). Licenses are contracts, which should be respected.

Royalty-Free (RF) licenses are cost-effective for businesses. However, the name "royalty-free" does not mean "free to use however you want." Always read the terms carefully, as there may still be limitations on use, distribution, or modification.

Rights-Managed (RM) licenses are more specific and limited. They are based on factors like duration of use, geographic area, and type of use. While often more expensive, they can be tailored to your specific needs. The catch? You need to track these licenses carefully to ensure you are in compliance.

Creative Commons (CC) licenses are attractive to businesses on a budget. The images are often free to use under specified conditions. There are different types of CC licenses, each with its own rules. Some require attribution to the creator, others allow modification but require you to share under the same license, some restrict commercial use, and others prohibit any modifications.

Public Domain images are not restricted. However, be cautious and confirm that the work is genuinely in the public domain before using it.

Understanding these license types is your first line of defense against claims of copyright infringement. It is the foundation upon which you will build your image sourcing strategy.

Resources for Licensed Images

Now that you understand the types of licenses, where can you find images to use? There are numerous sources.

Stock photo websites like Shutterstock, Getty Images, and Adobe Stock are popular choices. They offer a wide range of high-quality images with clear licensing terms. The downside? They can be costly, especially if you need images frequently.

If budget is a concern, consider free stock photo sites like Unsplash, Pexels, or Pixabay. These sources often offer images free for commercial use, though the quality and selection may be more limited than paid sites.

For those willing to put in a bit more legwork, Creative Commons search engines like CC Search or Flickr Creative Commons allow you to filter by license type.

Remember to always verify the license and provide proper attribution.

Do not overlook government resources. Many government agencies, like NASA, offer public domain images. Of course, ensure the images are not copyrighted by third parties.[13]

Finally, consider creating original content. Hiring photographers or illustrators, or using employee-created images can provide you with unique, branded imagery. While potentially more expensive upfront, it can offer long-term value and set you apart from competitors using the stock images.

---

[13] *See, e.g., Gaylord v. U.S.*, 595 F.3d 1364 (Fed. Cir. 2010) (Copyright infringement claim by sculptor against the U.S. government for using an image of his Korean War Veterans Memorial sculpture on a postage stamp without permission. The United States Court of Appeals for the Federal Circuit ruled that the government's use of the image on the stamp was not fair use and that the sculptor was entitled to compensation.).

When choosing your image resources, consider factors like image quality, licensing terms, pricing, and the specific needs of your project. The right mix of sources can help you create compelling visual content while managing your budget and copyright risks.

Proper Attribution and Record-Keeping

After sourcing your images, proper attribution and meticulous record-keeping are your next lines of defense against copyright issues.

When it comes to crediting image sources, follow the specific attribution requirements of each license. Typically, this includes the creator's name, title of the work, source URL, and license type. Place these credits in a visible location, either near the image or in a dedicated credits section.

Create a system for tracking image usage and licenses. This could be a digital asset management (DAM) system or even a well-organized spreadsheet. For each image, record key information like the source and creator, date acquired, license type and terms, expiration date (if applicable), and where and how the image is being used.

Do not forget to maintain documentation for legal compliance. Keep copies of license agreements and receipts. Consider printing or saving as PDF and make sure that the record reflects the scope of your permission and the work(s) that you are using. If you are using images under fair use, document your analysis. Retain these records even after you stop using an image. Copyright claims can arise after the fact, and good records might establish your best defense.

Regular audits of your image use are helpful. Conduct periodic reviews to ensure all images in use have proper licensing and attribution. Remove or replace images with expired licenses.

Remember, proper record-keeping is not just about preventing infringement. If you face a copyright claim, this documentation can be invaluable in demonstrating your good faith efforts to comply with copyright law.

Conducting Content Audits

Regular audits of your digital assets can catch potential issues before they become problems. Think of it as a health check-up for your content.

Develop a schedule for reviewing published content. Conduct thorough audits, with more frequent spot-checks for high-risk content areas.

During these audits, focus on identifying and addressing potential copyright issues.

Check that all images have proper licensing and attribution, verify that licenses have not expired, and ensure fair use claims are still valid.

Be prepared to update or remove content as necessary. Replace images with expired licenses, update attribution if creator information has changed, and remove content if you can no longer verify its copyright status.

Document your audit process thoroughly. Keep records of when audits were conducted and by whom, document any issues found and how they were resolved, and use these findings to improve your overall copyright compliance processes.

Regular audits demonstrate your commitment to copyright compliance and can help catch issues early, potentially saving you from costly legal battles down the line.

Leveraging Technology

As technology advances, new tools are emerging to help manage copyright compliance. While these should supplement rather than replace human oversight, they can aid your compliance efforts.

Consider exploring image recognition and tracking tools. Services like TinEye or Google Image Search can help you check image origins. Digital watermarking can protect your own images, and implementing reverse image search in your content workflow can help identify potential issues.

Automated copyright checks can be integrated into your processes. Look for plugins or software that check for proper image licensing during the upload process, or systems that flag potentially problematic uses for human review.

Artificial intelligence and machine learning are being used for content moderation. AI-powered tools can help identify copyrighted content in user-generated content, while machine learning can improve your tagging and categorization of digital assets.

Even blockchain technology is entering the copyright management space. Some platforms use blockchain to create immutable records of creation and licensing, which could revolutionize how we track and manage digital rights in the future.

While these technologies offer exciting possibilities, remember that they should enhance, not replace, your human-driven copyright compliance efforts.

Conclusion

Effective digital asset management is important for navigating the complex world of copyright in the digital age. By understanding licenses, sourcing images responsibly, keeping meticulous records, implementing robust systems, managing user content carefully, conducting regular audits, and leveraging technology, you can significantly reduce your risk of copyright infringement.

Remember, the goal is not to merely avoid legal issues. It is about fostering a culture of respect for intellectual property that enhances your brand's reputation and contributes to a healthier digital ecosystem. As you implement these best practices, you will find that good digital asset management not only protects your business but also improves your overall content strategy and operational efficiency.

In our journey through copyright challenges, we have now equipped ourselves with the tools to manage digital assets effectively. Copyright compliance, while sometimes challenging, can lead to unexpected avenues for growth and excellence in your business.

FINAL THOUGHTS

As a business owner, you pour your heart and soul into building your company. You craft your brand, develop your products, and work tirelessly to establish your presence in the market. But in today's digital age, where content is king and information flows freely, you might find yourself facing an unexpected threat: a copyright infringement claim.

Imagine the following hypothetical. It is a typical Monday morning. You are sipping your coffee, scrolling through your emails, when suddenly, your heart skips a beat. There it is—a cease-and-desist letter claiming your business infringed on someone's copyright. Your mind races. What does this mean for your company?

How did this happen? What should you do next?

First and foremost, take a deep breath. While this situation is serious, it is not the end of the world. Many businesses face copyright challenges, and with the right approach, you can navigate these waters successfully.

Start by understanding what you are up against. Copyright law is complex, but at its core, it protects original works of authorship. This could be anything from a photograph to a piece of software code.

That cease-and-desist letter in your inbox? It is a formal warning. It is the copyright holder's way of saying, "We think you are using our stuff without permission, and we want you to stop." While it can be intimidating, receiving this letter does not necessarily mean you are in the wrong or that you are being sued.

First, do not panic, but act promptly. Document everything related to the claim and preserve relevant evidence. This might include records of where you sourced the content in question or any licenses you believe give you the right to use the content.

Next, assess the situation. Is the claim valid? Could this be a misunderstanding? Sometimes, what seems like infringement might actually fall under fair use.

Engage a lawyer. A lawyer experienced in intellectual property can help you understand your position and options. These might include complying with the demand, negotiating with the copyright holder, disputing the claim, or in some cases, preparing for litigation.

If the situation escalates to litigation, understanding the process can help you feel more in control. From the initial complaint to the potential trial, each stage has its own challenges and opportunities. Your legal team will be important in developing a strategy, whether that involves presenting strong defenses or exploring settlement options.

The best way to handle copyright infringement claims is to prevent them from happening in the first place. This is where a robust copyright compliance policy comes into play. By implementing clear guidelines, providing regular training for your team, and establishing approval processes for content publication, you can significantly reduce your risk of infringement.

Keep in mind that balancing copyright compliance with creativity and innovation is key. Your goal should be to foster a culture where your team can create and innovate freely, while respecting the intellectual property rights of others.

Remember, staying informed is important. Copyright law and best practices are constantly evolving, especially in the digital age. Make a commitment to ongoing education and be ready to adapt your strategies as needed.

In the end, view copyright compliance not as a burden, but as an integral part of your business strategy. It is about protecting your assets, demonstrating respect for creativity, and positioning your company for long-term success in our content-driven world.

When you face a copyright challenge—whether it is a cease-and-desist letter in your inbox or a need to revamp your compliance policies—take a deep breath and approach it strategically.

PART 3

APPENDIX

ABOUT NICK GUINN

Nick is an intellectual property attorney as well as a speaker and author who presents on intellectual property topics.

Nick's expertise has led him to be a guest speaker across the country on intellectual property topics. To date, Nick has helped hundreds of clients around the world protect, enforce, and defend their copyrights and other intellectual property.

In 2021, Nick launched Coral Reef IP, a publishing venture founded on his passion for educating the public on copyrights and other IP topics. Coral Reef IP strives to educate businesses on IP topics relevant to them.

To learn more about Nick's speaking and publishing, visit NickGuinn.com. If you are looking for a content-rich, unique speaker for your in-person or virtual event or podcast, contact Nick for his speaker kit.

ALSO BY NICK GUINN

Presentations

The Totally Tubular TTAB Talk, TexasBarCLE: State Bar of Texas IP Section Annual Meeting, Dallas, Texas, June 2024.

Career Panel for Trademark Professionals, INTA's Annual Meeting, May 2024 (co-presented with Tamara Carmichael, Stacy Stewart, Lauren Burke, and Jeffrey Kobulnick).

Using and Rebutting Consumer Surveys, TexasBarCLE: Advanced Intellectual Property, February 2024.

North America Chapter, INTA's International Trademark Course, Fall 2023 (co-presented with Katy Basile, Amanda Hyland, and Brian Beverly).

223 Years Later: Journey of the U.S. Copyright Act, TexasBarCLE: State Bar of Texas IP Section Annual Meeting, Austin, Texas, June 2023.

Dispositive Motions, TexasBarCLE: Federal Court Practice Course, May 2023.

Fireside Chat—Insights from the Bench, TexasBarCLE: Advanced Intellectual Property Litigation, Dallas, Texas, February 2022 (moderator).

TexasBarCLE: Federal Court Practice Course, May 2021 (course director).

Brand Protection After Tiffany v. Costco, TexasBarCLE: Intellectual Property Law Workshop: Trademarks in IP, February 2021 (co-presented with Oren Gelber and Michael Moore).

A Rubric of Rights: Copyright and Trademark Protection for Fictional Characters, IIPLA Virtual IP Summit 2020, October 2020 (co-presented with Stephen J. Strauss and Alexandra Arneri).

Copyright Trolls: Ethical Issues, TexasBarCLE: 16th Annual Advanced Intellectual Property Litigation, Dallas, Texas, October 2020.

Trademark Trial and Appeal Board (TTAB) Practice, State Bar of Texas and USPTO: Virtual Trademark Bootcamp, June 2020.

What Should I Consider When Choosing a Trademark, State Bar of Texas and USPTO:

Virtual Trademark Bootcamp, June 2020 (co-presented with Stephanie Schmidt).

Trademark Applications Worth Talking About, TexasBarCLE: Intellectual Property Law Workshop: Trademarks in IP, February 2020.

UnReal Campaign Presentation (Counterfeiting Concerns), Clark High School, San Antonio, Texas, November 2019.

IP in Art or: How I learned to Stop Worrying and Love the Copyrights, City of San Antonio Department of Arts and Culture, San Antonio, Texas, November 2019.

Recent Trademark Issues in the News, HLSA, San Antonio, Texas, October 2019.

Litigating a Case with More than Just Patents, TexasBarCLE: 15th Annual Advanced Patent Litigation, San Antonio, Texas, July 2019.

Counterfeiting is Bigger than Handbags: Public Health and Economic Risks, Southwest Fulbright Symposium, San Antonio, Texas, April 2019.

Trademarks in Entertainment Law, Law Society for Sports, Entertainment, and Media, San Antonio, Texas, March 2019.

The Crossroads of Intellectual Property and Energy Law, Society of Oil and Gas Students, St.

Mary's University School of Law, San Antonio, Texas, March 2019.

Trademarks in Professional Sports, San Antonio Young Lawyers Association, AT&T Center, San Antonio, Texas, January 2019.

A Primer on Trademarks, Counterfeit Pharma Seminar, San Antonio, Texas, February 2018.

An Introduction to Trademarks, State Bar of Texas Pro Bono IP Workshop, El Paso, Texas, January 2018 (co-presented with Marylauren Ilagan).

Intellectual Property Basics, San Antonio Young Lawyers Association, San Antonio, Texas, October 2017.

Understanding and Communicating Intellectual Property: Means for Mitigating Barriers to Wealth, Southwest Fulbright Symposium, San Antonio, Texas, September 2017.

Impact of Apple v. Samsung on Design Patent Enforcement, TexasBarCLE: 13th Annual Advanced Patent Litigation, Horseshoe Bay, Texas, July 2017.

Intellectual Property Issues for Health Law Practitioners, San Antonio Bar Association Health Law Section, San Antonio, Texas, March 2017.

An Introduction to Trademarks, State Bar of Texas Pro Bono IP Workshop, Corpus Christi, Texas, January 2017 (co-presented with Darrian Campbell).

Learning to Protect Your Work, AIGA, San Antonio, Texas, November 2016.

How to Do a Pro Bono Clemency Petition, San Antonio Young Lawyers Association, San Antonio, Texas, September 2015.

Publications

The Staying Power of Trademarks, THE TRADEMARK LAWYER, Issue 2 2024, at 12–17.

Using and Rebutting Consumer Surveys, TexasBarCLE: Advanced Intellectual Property, February 2024.

PROTECT ENFORCE DEFEND: THE ULTIMATE GUIDE FOR ASPIRING IP LAWYERS (2022).

223 Years Later: Journey of the U.S. Copyright Act, TexasBarCLE: State Bar of Texas IP Section Annual Meeting, Austin, Texas, June 2023.

Dispositive Motions, TexasBarCLE: Federal Court Practice Course, May 2023.

EVERYTHING YOU ALWAYS WANTED TO KNOW ABOUT TRADEMARKS: THE ESSENTIAL GUIDE FOR ALL ONLINE BUSINESSES (2022).

Fireside Chat—Insights from the Bench, TexasBarCLE: Advanced Intellectual Property Litigation, Dallas, Texas, February 2022 (co-authored with the Honorable Xavier Rodriguez).

Brand Protection After Tiffany v. Costco, TexasBarCLE: Intellectual Property Law Workshop: Trademarks in IP, February 2021 (co-authored with Oren Gelber and Michael Moore).

Copyright Trolls: Ethical Issues, TexasBarCLE: 16th Annual Advanced Intellectual Property Litigation, October 2020.

Trademark Applications Worth Talking About, TexasBarCLE: Intellectual Property Law Workshop: Trademarks in IP, February 2020.

Litigating a Case with More than Just Patents, TexasBarCLE: 15th Annual Advanced Patent Litigation, July 2019.

Impressions of a TTAB Oral Argument Hearing From a First-Time Advocate, State Bar of Texas IP Section, Newsletter, August 2018 at 16–19.

Texas Supreme Court Update, State Bar of Texas Litigation Section, News for the Bar, November 2017.

Impact of Apple v. Samsung on Design Patent Enforcement, TexasBarCLE: 13th Annual Advanced Patent Litigation, July 2017.

Texas Supreme Court Update, State Bar of Texas Litigation Section, News for the Bar, June 2017.

Practical Trial & Motions Tips, San Antonio Bar Association Seminar: Bench Motions & Trials IX, May 2017 (co-authored with Judge Michael Mery).

Gorsuch's Appointment Could Affect the Deference Given to the USPTO Under Chevron and Auer, State Bar of Texas IP Section, Newsletter, May 2017 at 17–19.

Texas Supreme Court Update, State Bar of Texas Litigation Section, News for the Bar, March 2017.

Texas Supreme Court Update, State Bar of Texas Litigation Section, News for the Bar, November 2016.

CORALREEFIP

A Community for Innovators, Inventors, and Entrepreneurs

A SMALL REQUEST

Thank you for reading *Don't Copy & Paste*. I am positive that if you follow what I have written, you will be on your way to successfully avoiding and/or defending your business against copyright infringement claims.

I have a small, quick favor to ask.

Would you mind taking a minute and leaving an honest review on Amazon.com?

Reviews are the BEST way to help others purchase this book, and I check all my reviews looking for helpful feedback. Visit:

NickGuinn.com/reviews

A SPECIAL GIFT FOR READERS

I prepared a simple and helpful checklist you can download that gives you a list of common defenses that you might assert in response to a copyright infringement claim. You can access this checklist by visiting this website:

NickGuinn.com/resources

FREE DOWNLOAD

Made in the USA
Monee, IL
04 November 2026

67384093R00085